ZERO TO TEN

For my parents Lyn and Erich

Many thanks to the staff and children at
Flamingo Montessori Day Nursery, Burnham, Berkshire
and Teeny Tots Nursery, Slough, Berkshire
for their help and advice.

This edition published in 2002 by Zero to Ten Ltd.
327 High Street, Slough, Berkshire SL1 1TX, UK
and 814 North Franklin Street, Chicago Illinois 60610, USA

Reprinted 2004
Publisher: Anna McQuinn
Art Director: Tim Foster
Senior Art Editor: Sarah Godwin
Publishing Assistant: Vikram Parashar

A CIP catalogue record for this book is available from the British Library.

Library of Congress CIP data applied for.

ISBN 1-84089-172-6

Printed in Malta

Rainforest Animals

Illustrated by

Paul Hess

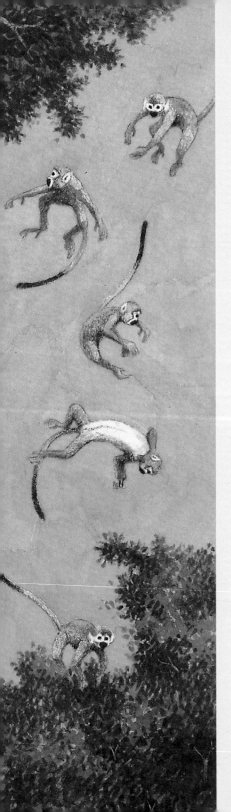

Monkey

IF YOU WANT TO CATCH A MONKEY
You're guaranteed to fail
Until you learn to leap from trees
While swinging by your tail.

Parrot

PURPLE, GREEN, RED, BLUE OR YELLOW
The parrot is a colourful fellow
He sits at the top of a tropical tree
And loudly squawks – "Hey, look at me!"

Anteater

THE ANTEATER'S A NOSY BEAST
With a sniffley, snuffley snoot;
He comes out at night for his evening feast,
A shuffling, whuffling brute.

Snake

DON'T EVER MAKE THE BAD MISTAKE
of stepping on the sleeping snake
because his jaws
might be awake.

Jaguar

THE JAGUAR IS WILD – SHE'S A JUNGLE CAT

With a frightfully loud sort of purr.

Her fine spotted coat

Gives her reason to gloat

And to spend the day licking her fur.

Toucan

WHATEVER ONE TOUCAN CAN DO
is sooner done by toucans two,
and three toucans (it's very true)
can do much more than two can do.

Tapir

THE TAPIR HAS NO MANNERS,

He picks food with his nose.

He swims and stomps the moonlit swamps,

With stubby little toes.

Tree Frog

"DEE DEEP," HE SAYS
And stops, till when
It's time to say
"Dee deep" again.

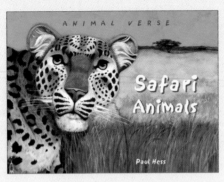
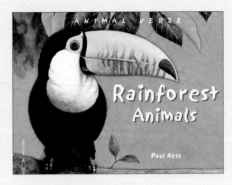

Farmyard Animals
ISBN 1-84089-170-X

Safari Animals
ISBN 1-84089-171-8

Rainforest Animals
ISBN 1-84089-172-6

Polar Animals
ISBN 1-84089-173-4

"SEARCH FOR THE ROCKET"

ZERO TO TEN publishes quality picture books for children aged between zero and ten!
Our books are available from all good bookstores.

If you have any problems obtaining any title, or would like to receive information about our books, please contact the publishers:
ZERO TO TEN 327 High Street, Slough, Berkshire SL1 1TX Tel: 01753 578 499 Fax: 01753 578 488 or
814 North Franklin Street, Chicago, Illinois 60610 Toll Free Order Tel: (800) 888-IPG1 (4741) All other inquiries: (312) 337 0747 Fax: (312) 337 5985